5 STEPS TO A PRODUCTIVE WEEK

CALENDAR HACKING

A Minimalist Approach to Time Management & Productivity Habits

CALEB W. MORAN

Copyright © 2021 by Caleb W. Moran

All Rights Reserved. No part of this book may be reproduced in any form without permission in writing from the author. Reviewers may quote brief passages in reviews.

ISBN: 978-1-7367606-0-4

Dedication

This book is dedicated to my wife Alicia and my kids: Jaiden, Gavin, Landon, Dylan, and Hadley. Because of you, I have spent decades learning how to prioritize my time, life, finances, and values. I strive to be everything I possibly can be to you and for you. Legacy is not something I desire to leave behind but something I want to raise and see flourish before my eyes.

To my wife, you are the fuel to my fire for more in life – never settling for just enough or good enough. Your love pushes me to go further, try harder, and live more intentionally every day.

To my kids, I wasted years "trying" to make a better life for you, which caused me to miss out on precious moments. That me is gone, and I enjoy intentionally investing my time into your individual lives – watching firsthand the amazing gifts that God has placed inside of each of you. Time with you is never wasted. You are my life, my purpose, and my legacy.

I would also like to dedicate this book to my mom and dad. I know that one day you will not be here on this earth anymore. I am so thankful for the years I have had and the years I will continue to share with you. Thank you for raising me to work hard and serve hard. Your example has allowed me to help thousands of others around the world. Your example of love and sacrifice has molded and shaped my life beyond measure. I am so thankful to be your son. I love you.

FREE GIFT FOR MY READERS:

I have a special gift for my readers! If you would like to get a FREE 20-minute *Calendar Hacking* session with me to see how we can improve your productivity and get back more of your time, book a call with me here:

Visit
www.CalendarHackingBook.com
to speak with Caleb

ALSO, JOIN THE FREE FACEBOOK GROUP NOW TO CONNECT WITH OTHER CALENDAR HACKERS:

Facebook.com/groups/CalendarHackingBook

Table of Contents

Introduction 1

My Pivotal Moment 5

The Mountain Climber Method 9

Boundaries... 13

The Two Most Important Distinctions 17

Step 1 | First Things First 21

Step 2 | Lock It In 37

Step 3 | List It or Miss It 43

Step 4 | Fill In The Slots 47

Step 5 | Nickle and Dime It 53

No White Space Allowed 61

My Secret Move 67

Adapt With The Seasons 71

Calendar Hacking Praise.. 77

What's the Forecast? 87

5 Steps to a Productive Week – Recap...................................... 91

Resources For Your Toolbox.. 93

About the Author 97

Notes 99

Introduction

Nothing is more draining, miserable, or unsettling than not having control of your own life.

Have you ever felt this way?

I'm willing to bet you have or you wouldn't have purchased this book. We've all been there – myself included – more times than we'd like to admit.

Your social-economic status and your geographical location don't matter because time can work for you or against you.

Life is lived one day at a time, and sadly, most people don't know how to manage their days properly and unintentionally take each day as it comes. This is often a Russian roulette approach – not knowing if today will be a good day or reflect previous days where nothing was accomplished or went as planned. No matter what your responsibilities are, they never seem to get done, or something always falls through the cracks because you don't have a straightforward and intentional plan.

It doesn't have to be that way.

What if I told you there is a hack that will give you back the seemingly lost time and help you intentionally complete your responsibilities while living your best life and nurturing what matters most to you – *your priorities*?

Well, there is! In this book, you will learn the *Calendar Hacking* method that I use with all of my clients to help them balance their career, family, personal life, relationships, health, finances, spirituality, and every other desire and goal lying dormant within them. This proven method works!

Years ago, I developed these five steps through much pain and anguish and tested them in my own life. Once I saw it take myself, my marriage, my family, my relationship with God, and my businesses to the next level – I was determined to share it with others. Today, it's your turn.

Get ready. You are just five steps away from UNDERwhelming your life and maximizing your days.

But wait, before turning the page and diving into the secret sauce for your success, I need you to start changing your mindset towards life in general – especially your daily routines and experiences. In the Bible, Proverbs 23:7 tells us in The Passion Translation, *"For as he thinks within himself, so is he."* So basically, it is telling us that our thoughts produce our outcome in life.

Mindset is a significant part of your success and must be tweaked daily.

Repeat after me, *"I can do this. I can balance my career and my family, and they can both be successful. I will not give up on myself or my goals and dreams because of disorganization or neglect. I will find a way to push through this season of my life, and I will become better."*

Now, doesn't that feel good? You will get out of this book what you put into it. Purchasing this book will not magically change your life, but if you let me coach you through these pages, you will begin to see results immediately, and you will find that you have way more time on your hands than you ever did before.

In the following chapters, I will share some of my life's lowest moments that brought me to some of my highest moments. Just think, you've had control this whole time and didn't know it. With this new knowledge and the simplicity of the steps and application, you will begin to see momentum gain and progress appear. Let's do it!

My Pivotal Moment

"Time is the coin of your life. It is the only coin you have, and only you can determine how it will be spent. Be careful lest you let other people spend it for you."
—Carl Sandburg

"Not right now…"

I'll never forget this day for the rest of my life. It's a day I'm not proud of, but I learned from it and hope you can as well.

My wife and I had just launched out as entrepreneurs. We were quickly growing our family and had three amazing boys at home. I worked out of my house, so I was home ALL the time, but more so presently absent. Even though I was there, I needed my family to pretend that I wasn't. If you're an entrepreneur reading this, you know exactly what I mean. The entrepreneurship grind is exhilarating but can become daunting if you aren't careful.

I have always endeavored to be an active and involved parent in my kids' lives. The stress of my new businesses was wearing on me. (Yes, I said businesses plural. I was running two full-time businesses simultaneously.) Any noise in the house set off frustration sensors in every fiber of my being. I lived on the offense – quick to snap at anyone who bothered me or interrupted my work. The saddest part of it all was that I was operating on two hours of sleep per night and working ALL the time. That meant that my kids were on pins and needles ALL day because daddy was always working.

One night, my oldest son came over to me at the dining room table (also known as my office) and asked me if I would like to throw the football. With a frustrated smile, I gained my composure and said, *"Hey buddy, Daddy would love to. Just let me finish my client's project, then we can go outside and throw the ball."* He agreed and turned and walked away as I resumed my work.

Later (how much later, I have no idea), he came back and asked me, *"Hey Daddy, are you done working yet so we can throw the football?"* I looked up from my laptop and said, *"Son, daddy has to finish this project first. As soon as I finish, we will throw the ball."*

He walked away, and I continued the grind. I bet you know where this story is going. Maybe it hits home for you and your life? Did we have kids only to put up walls of work and responsibility around us that cause us to unintentionally avoid them while juggling all the things in life that are overwhelming us?

He asked me again, and my answer was the same. When I finally finished the project, I slammed the laptop shut and quickly pushed myself away from the table, ready to throw the football with my son.

As I started to call out his name, I caught a glimpse of him on the couch. He was asleep. I looked at the clock on the microwave, and it was 4:00 AM. What??!! Had I been so engulfed in my job that time seemed the be lost, and I was in another dimension? I walked over and kissed my son on his head, only to find his tiny arms wrapped around his football. I broke down and started crying. *"What kind of father am I?"* I asked myself. I could try to justify it because I was doing it all for him, right? But is that how he saw it? Is that how he felt about his dad? Was I the hardworking dad trying to make all of his dreams come true, or was I the presently absent father who was there but not really there? I had so much on my plate and had no clue how to manage or change it. Have you been there before? Maybe you know someone who is there right now.

These moments of extreme pain in my life forced me to make changes that helped me pivot toward a direction and destination that I desired to be but had no clue how to get there.

This is how I developed *Calendar Hacking*.

The Mountain Climber Method

*"Great achievement is usually born of great sacrifice
and is never the result of selfishness."*
–Napoleon Hill

I remember hearing stories about people who set out to climb some of the world's highest mountains. I have climbed small mountains but never had to train or pack for them.

If you are an avid mountain climber, forgive me now for anything said beyond this sentence that may not accurately depict mountain climbing. But we'll use this story as an analogy to help you understand what we will be talking about concerning balancing your life.

Usually, climbers start on the long treks up mountains with a lot more gear and supplies than when they finish. Base camps are set up at certain altitudes so that a climber can wait there – sometimes overnight – until their body acclimates to the higher altitude. Typically, a climber has a tent, pots and pans, and a few other essentials to use at the campsite. When their body is fully acclimated, they must decide what supplies to take or leave behind before continuing to climb.

The higher they climb, the more difficult it will be to lug around unnecessary items, so they must take only the essentials needed. This process repeats at each base camp as the climber ascends and acclimates. Climbers must decide what to give up to go up.

"Our life is the sum total of all the decisions we make every day, and those decisions are determined by our priorities."
–Myles Munroe

As an executive coach, I find my clients often come to me with a vast array of extras in their lives – especially their daily routines. As we begin discussing their daily routines and habits, the conversation usually comes to a screeching halt.

You cannot do everything and do it all 100%.

I had to learn this the hard way. My mother and father were both entrepreneurs with an extreme work ethic and drive. There wasn't much they couldn't do, and they did what they could with little sleep (which is where I got it from). This schedule works for a season, but eventually, it can become a cycle of bad decisions and choices made in your life that cause you to arrive at a destination you never intended.

Does this sound familiar to you?

Are you at a place right now that might be unhealthy for you, your family, your career – or even your mental health if you don't make a change soon? Well, don't worry – I got you. Things are about to become a lot less overwhelming for you. What you are about to learn will UNDERwhelm your seemingly overwhelmed life.

Where was I?

Ah yes, giving up to go up and how I help my clients. Let's continue. If you truly desire change, it will require a change to get it. Mike Murdock once said:

"The secret of your future is hidden in your daily routine."

Your daily actions are a forecast of your future. Today determines tomorrow.

- Have you ever tried to live a day intentionally?

- Have you ever made a schedule and done nothing else but what was on your calendar?

Setting boundaries around how you spend your time each day will liberate and protect you. Someone who allows their time to be eaten up by anything and everything that demands it is a toxin to themselves, their family, and their business.

I saw a recent documentary showcasing two brothers who took the path of becoming minimalists. One day they decided to pack the contents of their entire house into boxes. Every single item in the house went into a box and was moved to storage. For 30 days, if either brother needed anything from the boxes, he could get it. After 30 days, any items remaining in the boxes were donated to charity, given away, or thrown out because they weren't important to daily life. Wow, that's a dramatic approach to getting your life in order.

Can you imagine? Right now, I bet you are thinking about all the things in your attic that you haven't looked at or needed for years – possibly decades. These many items that you feel you need aren't helping your everyday life. What if you chose to give them up to go up? What if you decide to leave these at the base camp of who you have always been to become who you have always desired to be?

This is exactly what we will be doing with *Calendar Hacking*. Put everything you do in a box. Well, not an actual box, but let's assume you have a clean slate. You can now choose what happens in your day and when it happens. Feels liberating, huh? Well, it is. You are the master of your day – not your kids, spouse, boss, career, clients, or even your responsibilities. You get to choose now, so what will you choose? Let's dive into these proven five steps and see how to UNDERwhelm an overwhelming life. Throughout these steps, you will hear some praise from people who have seen first-hand the transformative power of these five steps.

Boundaries

"Every human being must have boundaries in order to have successful relationships or a successful performance in life."
–Henry Cloud

You can plan all you want, but you will never accomplish what you schedule and set out to do without boundaries.

Boundaries are all around us.

The roads we drive on have painted lines, creating lanes for drivers to travel safely to their destination. We live in houses with fences that protect us by preventing intruders from entering the property. As children, we learn boundaries at school – which side of the hall to walk on, how we should address our superiors, policies and procedures for assignments, tests, exams, and even correction and reprimand when needed. Almost everything we are a part of in our culture has boundaries that keep everything operating the way it should.

Why is it we rarely find boundaries in our calendars and the way we manage our time?

One of my clients was complaining about feeling as if she never accomplished anything. She said, *"It seems like I spend all day on the phone with people but never really get anywhere. Before I know it, the day is over, I have not made any sales, and my company* has not advanced. I am putting so much time and effort in, but I do not see a return."* As a coach, I see this often. While it may be a normal occurrence, it is a form of neglect.

I told her, *"The issue is that you are **spending** more time than you are **investing**. You must learn to evaluate your time and eliminate unneeded and unwanted things that are draining it. You need boundaries. You do not have to answer every text or reply to every email. You do not have to give yourself to everything and everyone who demands of you when it is convenient for them. You must place a boundary that causes them to navigate their relationship with you inside those boundary lines."*

Dr. Henry Cloud, in his book "Boundaries" said it like this:

> *"Part of taking responsibility, or ownership, is knowing what is our job, and what isn't."*

Sounds simple, but man is it hard. As a husband, I have to know what only I can do in my marriage. As a father, I have to know what only I can do and be in my children's lives. As an entrepreneur and leader, I must stay in my lane with my team and my clients to have all parties arrive at the desired destination.

Imagine if I asked you to take a road trip with me, but only I knew where we were going. If I chose to pick up every pedestrian we passed and asked them to drive us wherever they chose, we would never arrive at our destination. While this may seem a bit extreme, it is precisely what most people do with their time and relationships. You commonly see this with moms.

Women are nurturers by design – God made them that way. They will stop cooking dinner to coddle a sad child, put a Band-Aid on a skinned knee, or answer the phone and talk to an old friend. Once the task that demanded their time is complete, they go back to cooking dinner. I am not faulting women or isolating them from men. Men have their issues, too – usually worse. However, if you are a woman or at least grew up with one in your home, you know just how true this is.

So, what do we do?

First, you must learn the art of saying *"NO"* **or** *"NOT NOW"* **and experience the freedom that brings.**

Dr. Henry Cloud also said in his book:

> *"Functional boundaries refers to a person's ability to complete a task, project, or job. It has to do with performance, discipline, initiative, and planning. Relational boundaries refers to the ability to speak truth to others with whom we are in relationship."*

We must learn how to have functional and relational boundaries and set our priorities and goals to accomplish what we have set out to do.

People with boundary problems usually display extreme personalities or character traits like procrastination, micromanaging, control, manipulation, and the list goes on. Once you set boundaries, you and others will clearly understand where the relationship or task can or cannot go.

In the United States, every state has a boundary called the *state line*. Those state lines create jurisdiction for law enforcement and other legalities. Within every state, there are cities, towns, and villages that all have boundary lines. These boundaries separate *and* unite, which is why this country is called the United States of America. With proper boundaries in your life, you will not let someone waste the time allotted to accomplish something else. You will be able to unite all the necessary pieces in your day to achieve a task or goal.

I am a musician. One instrument that I love playing is the piano. When played correctly, the piano creates the most beautiful sounds to hear. But when not played correctly, the sound can be annoying. The reason for both the beauty and tragedy of this instrument's sounds is boundaries. Every key on the piano fits within a scale. If you play the wrong key in a scale, then the entire piece of music is tainted. As you learn to manage your time and calendar correctly, your life's sound will be music to your ears. If you remove boundaries or refuse to set them, your life will sound like turning a radio knob to random stations and never settling on any of them.

The Two Most Important Distinctions

Most people struggle with maintaining their calendars and managing their time. I will teach you and help you distinguish between priorities and responsibilities, which other time management books won't show you. It's imperative that you know and understand this to become a *Calendar Hacking* pro.

When I first meet with a client, I ask them to make a list of their priorities. This eye-opening exercise reveals the client's state of mind and how I will help coach them out of it.

For example, a debriefing of one client's day sounded like this: *"Well, I have a lot on my plate. I have to take the kids to school, go to work, pick the kids up from school, cook dinner, take them to soccer practice, and drop another kid off at ballet. Then, I quickly go to the grocery store while my kids are at practice, return to pick up kids, go home, do homework, put kids to bed, do laundry and help with other household chores. Then, tomorrow I repeat everything."*

Does this routine sound familiar to you?

Well, let's evaluate this for a moment. Is grocery shopping a priority or a responsibility, and what is the difference between the two?

The dictionary defines *priority* **as:** *Highest or higher in importance, rank, privilege, etc.*

Based on that definition, you can determine a priority by its level of importance in your life. Many people make a to-do list and prioritize their responsibilities or anything that needs to be taken care of urgently. However, this book will not teach you how to prioritize your responsibilities. You will learn what matters the most to you in life and how to make sure you invest your time and energy in those things.

Before we continue expounding on priorities, we need to see how responsibility is defined.

The dictionary defines *responsibility* **as:** *A particular burden of obligation upon one who is responsible.*

You see that a priority is something of high importance to you and a responsibility is a task you must carry out because you are accountable for it. So, as a husband and father of five kids, grocery shopping is not a priority; it is a responsibility. Investing time in my marriage or my kids is not a responsibility; it is a priority. My family is not a burden or a task. They are my life, my everything, and the reason I exist. Therefore, they must be a priority to me so that nothing else takes away from the time we invest as a family. Remember, any time you have with your family should be valued and seen as an investment and not an expense.

Now, there are times when a person's analytical brain overtakes this process and attempts to complicate the simplistic and minimalistic approach that we are taking. For instance, my kids are a priority of mine.

In the next chapter, I will show you an example of some of my priorities, but for now, I want you to understand how NOT to complicate your priorities.

As a priority, I invest time in my kids. One way to do this is a scheduled event like family night that gets put on my calendar to fulfill my priority. But what about driving my kids to school? Is that a priority since my kids are a priority? No. It is not. It is a responsibility that I am tasked with because I am their parent. So, I have to schedule that responsibility in my calendar and fulfill my obligation to it. Do you see how that is not a scheduled event centered around my priority?

In Step 5 of the *Five Steps to a Productive Week,* I will teach you the power of being intentional and milking your day for everything it's worth. So, you can invest in your relationship by being intentional while driving your kids to school.

Don't assume that distinguishing between priorities and responsibilities is too complicated. When it comes to priorities, I have yet to find a client who had more than ten priorities once we really boiled everything down to what matters the most in life to them.

With this in mind, let me give you a brief overview of what is included in the chapters ahead that will UNDERwhelm your life and help maximize and monetize your calendar. You will learn how to:

- Make a list of your priorities
- Spread those priorities throughout your week
- Schedule your priorities into your calendar
- Make a list of your responsibilities
- Fill all available time slots on your calendar with your responsibilities
- Schedule your responsibilities
- Get the most out of your day by hunting down any other available moments and directing them towards a priority

Step 1 | First Things First

> *"Decide what you want, decide what you are willing to exchange for it. Establish your priorities and go to work."*
> –H. L. Hunt

Your desire to invest in bettering yourself will pay huge dividends in the end. You are valuable and adding more value to yourself is always a good thing. Again, you know that, or you wouldn't have purchased this book.

As an executive coach, one of the reoccurring statements I hear from clients is, *"I am overwhelmed with all that I have to do and don't know how to get it all done."*

Let's face it; we've all been there. Today's pace is not like it was twenty years ago. With the continual uprising and advancements of technology, we continue to find more efficient ways to do things and reduce time. While this sounds good, it often makes room for us to pile more on our plates, and then we must try to prioritize ourselves in a technology-driven world. So, how do we take the same twenty-four hours in a day and make them as productive as other successful people around us? Steven Covey once said:

> *"The key is not to prioritize what's on your schedule, but to schedule your priorities."*

Being a father of five, running multiple businesses, overseeing a network of hundreds of non-profits, traveling and speaking at conferences worldwide, staying involved in my community and state, operating a coaching company, while trying to find time to go to the gym and cultivate relationships with friends, I have to find time to fit in a breath or two.

So, how do we do this?

It's not as complex or overwhelming as it seems. The proven steps in this process are scalable to anyone's life; however, you must be determined to get it done. Again, you are valuable. Reading books like this is one way to invest in yourself and discover your worth.

Let's face it, we all have a lot to do in seemingly little time. It's often easier to execute things in steps, so this is why I've developed these FIVE PROVEN STEPS to help you UNDERwhelm a seemingly overwhelming life load.

Step One sets the stage for the entire week, and ultimately the culture of your life. First, you need to **make a list of your priorities**. Yes, priorities.

It's too easy to take life as it comes, doing whatever demands your time at the moment.

John C. Maxwell once said,

> "Time management is an oxymoron. Time is beyond our control, and the clock keeps ticking regardless of how we lead our lives. Priority management is the answer to maximizing the time we have."

I couldn't agree more. So many people try to manage their time but forget about their priorities. So, as a business owner, I had to learn to treat my time like clients. I cannot spend time with all my clients at once, so I must devote specific times or days to them. Once you have determined what **MUST** happen in your day or week, this will help you know how to spread it out over the weekdays (in the next step, I provide an example of a scheduled workweek). Elisabeth Hasselbeck once said,

> "Nobody's life is ever all balanced. It's a conscious decision to choose your priorities every day."

For instance, it is a priority for me to provide for my family. That means I must schedule time to be at work and grow my businesses and staff. Another priority of mine is my marriage and family. Family time and a date night must happen for me, so I intentionally schedule them into my week. While these cannot occur on the same day (for me at least), I schedule them on different days during the week.

Fitness and exercise are also a priority of mine. Because my days are long and grueling, I find working out early in the morning is easiest for me and my schedule. It's not fun waking up early to work out, but it's a priority, and I must give it an intentional time slot in my day. You will notice throughout this book that I use the word *intentional* a lot. That's because you have to be intentional with your time if you desire to get something from it. Every good investment has a positive ROI.

Reading and educating myself is another priority that I have, so I must have a place for that in my day as well. I used to say, *"I don't have time to read books. I'm so busy."* That's because, at the time, I valued sleep and watching TV to unwind over my desire to grow and expand my capacity and influence as a leader.

I am a Christian. Prayer and reading my bible is a major priority for me, so I make time for it. Men and women may have different daily/weekly responsibilities, but we must focus on priorities first over responsibilities. Train yourself not to think of everything that you have to do. Instead, in this step, think only about the things that you desire to do. You will find that what you value most will get the most attention. You'll begin to find creative ways to accomplish your goals and invest in your priorities.

Priorities are just that – *priority*. What we value the most should get the most of us.

Prioritize what matters the most to you.

We need to learn priority management and not only time management.

Remember, priorities will have to fall into a time slot, so managing that time is essential.

Good time management doesn't mean you do more, it means you do more of what matters most.

Craig Groeschel once said,

> *"The difference between the values you embrace and the life you live equals the frustration you experience."*

Once you determine what is non-negotiable in your week/life, those must be the first things that get scheduled on your calendar. Your week will affect your month, your month will set your quarter, and your quarter will predict your year. Invest your best in what matters most.

As I mentioned, I am blessed with five wonderful kids. A few years ago, my youngest son began to display symptoms that the doctor diagnosed as Mononucleosis. We left for a beach vacation and kept an eye on him that week to make sure he took it easy and got plenty of rest. When we returned home, my wife and I immediately had to repack our bags and head out to a conference where I was speaking. I took my son in a separate car with me, and my wife came later that night in her car with our four other children. As I got closer to our destination, I noticed my son wasn't acting right. His lips were blue, and he said weird things as he tried to keep his eyes open. Once we arrived, I lifted him out of my truck. He felt different, sounded different, and looked different. We couldn't shake the feeling that something more was wrong with him than the Mono diagnosis we were given, so we took him to the ER. What came next changed our lives – and his – forever. Blood tests revealed that he had Leukemia. We were immediately put in an ambulance and rushed back to our hometown to a hospital that could better treat our son's needs.

When we arrived, the doctors immediately took him into surgery to prepare him for chemotherapy by inserting a pic line into his heart. They told us this is a routine procedure, and he would be done and awake from sedation in about thirty minutes. We quickly kissed him, prayed over him, and waved to him as they rolled him away to surgery.

While attempting to wake him from sedation after the surgery, his lungs collapsed. A chest x-ray revealed a football-size tumor in his little three-year-old chest. Doctors immediately put him into a medically induced coma for an entire month. As I sat at the foot of his bed that first night, the doctor told me that my son wouldn't make it to the end of the week. You know what wasn't going through my head at that time? All my responsibilities. I didn't care who locked up the office or not that day. I wasn't worried about which one of my staff members was late to work or who hadn't finished their assignments for the projects or events we had coming up. I didn't even care if I had paid my cable, electricity, or water bills. My house could burn down, and it wouldn't have phased me one bit. I was thinking about my son.

I was told I had four days with my child, who couldn't see, hear, or talk back to me because he was in a coma. I began wondering not about the coming four days but the previous three years with my son.

Had I fathered him enough? Did I love him enough? Did I spend enough time with him, throw the ball with him, show him how much I loved him, and pour enough of myself into him in those three short years?

Sadly, the answer was no. I hadn't.

Phoebe Snow once said,

"Sometimes when you're overwhelmed by a situation – when you're in the darkest of darkness – that's when your priorities are reordered."

I had allowed the hundreds of responsibilities to choke out a priority that meant more to me than anything else in this world. I decided at that moment that this would never happen again. So, I began to reevaluate and take inventory of my calendar and time.

Maybe your life and situation aren't as dramatic as my story, but if your life came to a halt due to an unforeseen challenge, what would matter most to you?

When I take my clients through this exercise, 99% do not know the difference between a priority and a responsibility.

Let me help you out.

- Grocery shopping is a *responsibility*.
- Spending time with my family is a *priority*.
- Paying bills is a *responsibility*.
- Investing in my marriage is a *priority*.
- Bathing the dog is a *responsibility*.
- Taking care of my health and fitness is a *priority*.

See the difference?

Take a moment to reflect on what you think your priorities are. Pretend you have nothing else to do in a week – remove all your responsibilities as if they do not exist. Give yourself a clean slate. What do you want to invest your time into the most? Write those things down as priorities.

Actress Mariska Hargitay said it this way,

"Sometimes things in life happen that allow us to understand our priorities very clearly. Ultimately you can see those as gifts."

My Priorities

1. God
2. Marriage
3. Family
4. Personal Growth
5. Career
6. Fitness

Now it's your turn. On the next page, list the things that matter the most to you in life that you want to ensure are scheduled on your calendar and not neglected due to poor time management.

Your Priorities

What are your priorities – the things you value the most that must fit into your week? List them below:

_____   _____

_____   _____

_____   _____

_____   _____

_____   _____

Once you determine and list your priorities, you need to then dive into each one and determine *how* you will prioritize each one in your calendar. Simply listing a priority will not accomplish that task. You cannot say that family time is a priority if you do not understand *how* you will achieve that time with your family.

For instance, if growing in your relationship with God is a priority, you may accomplish that by:

- Reading your bible
- Praying
- Going to church
- Attending a bible study
- Reading books on the topic of Christianity

One day, I was reviewing a client's priorities with him. After he determined what they were and wrote them down, I asked him, *"So how will you make these a priority in your calendar?"* With a puzzled look on his face, he timidly looked at me and said, *"Well, I'm not sure."*

I started with the first item on his priority list – God. I said, *"So, if your relationship with God is a priority, how will we get God into your calendar?"* Again, he said, *"Man, I'm not sure. I've always wanted to have a better relationship with God but have never known how to accomplish that."* So, I asked, *"Do you go to church?"* *"I want to go more and make it a priority in my life,"* he replied. *"Well, what time does your church hold its weekly services?"* I asked. *"There are a few service options on Sundays. 11:00 AM is the service that would best fit my family's needs. With as many kids as we have and one of them being an infant, waking them up early and getting them ready would be a real challenge right now,"* he replied.

With a smile on my face, I said, *"Well, then this is one way you make God a priority in your calendar. Get your phone out and schedule every Sunday at 11:00 AM into your phone. Set it to repeat weekly and set two alarms as a reminder – one an hour before and the second one 30 minutes before. This will help ensure you do not forget and will prompt you when you need to leave the house to arrive on time."*

We continued to discuss other things he wanted to do to help him make his relationship with God a priority. I asked him, *"Do you desire to read your Bible? If so, how often would you like to read it?"* *"Yes, but I've never been disciplined enough to do it. I would say a realistic goal would be to read my Bible three times a week,"* he said with excitement. So, we determined that Monday, Wednesday, and Friday would be the best days to spread that priority throughout his week. He chose 6:00 AM as his time slot and was so excited to see that his priority was now a reality. It's honestly that simple. Don't complicate things. Refuse to allow timidity or procrastination to prevent you from establishing and executing a priority.

If your priority is your marriage, *how* will you make it a priority in your calendar? Maybe you will have a scheduled weekly date night, a scheduled quarterly weekend getaway for just the two of you, or perhaps you will read books about marriage in the morning before going to the gym, attending marriage conferences, etc. You can see how determining a priority is one step but planning *how* you will make it a priority is another. On the next few pages, take some time and write down your action plan to accomplish each priority.

PRIORITY #1 _____

Plan of Action

_____
_____
_____
_____

PRIORITY #2 _____

Plan of Action

_____
_____
_____
_____

PRIORITY #3 _____

Plan of Action

_____
_____
_____
_____

PRIORITY #4 _____

Plan of Action

_____
_____
_____
_____

PRIORITY #5 _____

Plan of Action

_____
_____
_____
_____

PRIORITY #6 _____

Plan of Action

_____
_____
_____
_____

PRIORITY #7 _____

Plan of Action

_____
_____
_____
_____

PRIORITY #8 _____

Plan of Action

_____
_____
_____
_____

PRIORITY #9 _____

Plan of Action

_____
_____
_____
_____

PRIORITY #10 _____

Plan of Action

_____
_____
_____
_____

Step 2 | Lock It In

*"Don't be fooled by the calendar.
There are only as many days in the year as you make use of."*
—Charles Richards

It's one thing to make a list of things you hold near and dear to your heart and life; it's another thing to intentionally make sure those things get put into your daily, weekly, and monthly agenda. After determining your priorities, you need to spread them throughout your week by assigning them a time slot and intentionally scheduling them in your calendar.

Adjust your mindset and make your calendar an authority in your life. If it is in your calendar, YOU MUST OBEY IT!!!

Your calendar is your new boss.

I schedule everything in the calendar app on my smartphone, which syncs with my iPad, laptop, desktop, and other devices. Since my phone is always with me, my calendar is also. I also set two alarms for each event I schedule so that my phone prompts me about the scheduled event so I can adequately prepare for it.

I wear many hats on different days of the week, so my priorities must be divvied up throughout my week to ensure they get the attention and nurturing they need. For example, years ago, I came home after working a 115-hour week and was completely exhausted. Judging by the look on my wife's face as she watched two kids in diapers running amok – she was too. We desperately needed time away for her and me to reconnect as a married couple – but there seemingly was no time. Work had eaten up my entire week, and now I had to come home and work on my second job deep into the night. With tears in my eyes, I looked at my wife and said, "Babe, I am sorry that I don't have the money to take you shopping or to get away for the weekend, just the two of us. I am sorry that I work so much, and you are here at the house with the kids, tackling all the house responsibilities by yourself. One day we will be out of this season, but we MUST set aside time for us to be together until then. We have to make our marriage a priority."

I began to get creative. The bottom floor apartment we lived in overlooked a beautiful pond surrounded by a walking trail. When we put the kids down for bed later that night, I set a baby monitor in the room, grabbed a blanket, and took my wife by the hand as I pulled her outside. There, under the stars, getting eaten by the Louisiana mosquitos, we both exhaled a sigh of relief as we invested in one another and our relationship.

We were twenty feet from our kids' room, but it felt like we were on another planet. We talked about what our house would look like when we finally got out of the apartment life. We discussed the dream vacation we would take when we finally had the money to do something. We sat there for every bit of 20 minutes (because we felt guilty not being with the kids, ha-ha) and started making each other a priority. And you know what? It didn't cost me a dime. Many people procrastinate on the things that mean the most and need the most attention because they feel they don't have money or resources to tend to them. That could not be any further from the truth. As the father of five kids, sometimes stepping outside to stare at a tree for five minutes by myself is bliss.

It is important to understand that you *CANNOT* cancel a priority. You can reschedule one, but you cannot cancel it. Your calendar is boss. If your boss told you to meet with a colleague about a project on Thursday at 9:00 AM, but you had something come up, you would reschedule that meeting for later in the day or another day that week. You would not cancel it because of scheduling conflict, especially if your boss said it had to be done. Again, the primary reason priorities are overlooked is there are so many responsibilities that consume our minds and time. So, if my date night with my wife collided with a family funeral, I would reschedule my date night for Sunday evening instead of cancelling it on Thursday.

You can cancel a **responsibility** if needed but you *CANNOT* and should not cancel a **priority**. Do everything within your power to be faithful to your priorities.

Below is an example of some priorities spread throughout the week. You will notice that some time slots are empty; we will address those in the next few steps. I am self-employed, so my work week is not the average 9 to 5, Monday through Friday. I have multiple companies, and my work times are sporadically organized throughout the week. Your week and calendar will likely look different, but this is just an example for you to see how *Calendar Hacking* works. It is not a detailed look at my calendar (that would definitely overwhelm you).

MONDAY

5:00 AM-6:00 AM	Fitness (Gym)
6:00 AM-7:00 AM	Reading/Prayer
8:30 AM-2:30 PM	Work

TUESDAY

5:00 AM-6:00 AM	Fitness (Run
6:00 AM-7:00 AM	Reading/Prayer
8:30 AM-2:30 PM	Work

WEDNESDAY

5:00 AM-6:00 AM	Fitness (Gym)
6:00 AM-7:00 AM	Reading/Prayer
8:30 AM-2:30 PM	Work

THURSDAY

5:00 AM-6:00 AM	Fitness (Run)
6:00 AM-7:00 AM	Reading/Prayer
8:30 AM-2:30 PM	Work
5:00 PM-10:00 PM	Date Night

FRIDAY

5:00 AM-6:00 AM   Fitness (Gym)

6:00 AM-7:00 AM   Reading/Prayer

5:00 PM-10:00 PM   Family Night

SATURDAY

- This is a day I devote to my family, errands, honey-do's, and occasionally relaxing.
- This is a very unscheduled day on purpose, and I love it.

SUNDAY

- My family and I are involved in church, so we set Sundays aside for that as well as family time, errands, honey-do's, and some occasional relaxing.

As you can see, this looks easy; however, this is *NOT* all I do every day. This is only a list of my priorities. We will discuss responsibilities in the next chapter.

When you make priorities first, everything else will fall in line.

Step 3 | List It or Miss It

*"You cannot escape the responsibility of
tomorrow by evading it today."*
–Abraham Lincoln

Now that the most important things have been determined and intentionally scheduled in your calendar, you must list all of your responsibilities – both large and small.

With five kids, someone must take them to school, pick them up, take them to sports practices, music lessons, dance classes, etc.

Overwhelming tasks that used to get in the way of your priorities no longer will because now you know the proven *Calendar Hacking* method. Let me explain.

There are many things that I must do as an entrepreneur, husband, father, friend. However, these WILL NOT get in the way of my priorities. That is a boundary and non-negotiable decision that I had to make, and you will have to make it also.

I never want to tell my wife or children that I can't spend time with them because there are too many emails to check or clothes to take to the dry cleaners. Sounds comical, right? But sadly, it is most people's reality. Responsibilities cannot fall to the wayside, though, which is why this step is so important.

In this step, you will list everything else that you know has to happen in your week, such as the following activities:

- Take kids to/from school
- Domestic responsibilities / Honey-do's
- PTA meetings
- Volunteer work
- Doctor appointments
- Sports and hobbies
- Dry cleaning
- Errands
- Grocery shopping
- Pay bills
- Do taxes
- Walk the dog
- Get a haircut
- Get nails done
- Balance the checkbook
- Check the mail
- Cultivating relationships / social life
- Study for a test/exam
- Water the plants
- Feed the pets

List of Responsibilities

What are your responsibilities – the things you know must get done or all hell will break loose? List them below:

_____   _____

_____   _____

_____   _____

_____   _____

_____   _____

_____   _____

_____   _____

_____   _____

_____   _____

_____   _____

_____   _____

Responsibilities typically take up far more of our week than our priorities. If we aren't careful, responsibilities will choke out priorities the majority of the time.

Louie Giglio once said:

"Whenever you say yes to anything, there is less of you for something else. Make sure your yes is worth the less."

We cannot neglect our responsibilities. Making a detailed list will help to ensure nothing gets overlooked or left out.

Taking time to inventory and audit your daily routines will reveal areas that may be imbalanced or out of control. When you can lay everything out in front of you and see it for yourself, it is much easier to organize and categorize things.

If you are an entrepreneur like me, you have more freedom to move your calendar around to better serve your needs. If not, there are still some hours in the day you can control, so this is where you exercise your authority. In the next step, you will see precisely how to do this.

Step 4 | Fill In The Slots

"Some people want it to happen, some wish it would happen, others make it happen." –Michael Jordan

After intentionally scheduling what matters most in life to you (priorities), you must now schedule everything you know you must do. You will quickly see that your schedule has many available and unscheduled time slots. You must fill every one of these slots to ensure you accomplish what you are responsible for in your days and week.

You cannot go about this timidly; you must be aggressive during this step.

I'm reminded of a scene from "Scarface." (*I'm not advocating violence nor suggesting my approval of you watching this movie – but many of us have heard of or seen the scene from this movie.*) Actor Al Pacino holds an assault rifle with a grenade launcher in his hands and says, *"Say hello to my little friend!"* then begins to shoot up the entire room, hitting anything and everything in his line of sight.

Again, I'm not advocating violence or crime, but this is a picture of just how radically determined and aggressive you will need to be when putting your responsibilities on the calendar. Think about your responsibilities as bullets in a gun. With everything you have on your plate, load your gun, look at your calendar and say, *"Say hello to my little friend!"*

Okay, I think you get my point. All I am saying is, you now need to get very serious about executing your week. You have to put every responsibility in an open time slot, ensuring everything in your line of sight gets a responsibility.

Notice that you do not need to try to do everything in one day? That's impossible and overwhelming.

Once you have set your priorities throughout the week, you now have time slots to pepper your other responsibilities and needs throughout – enabling you to slay your week with your so-called assault rifle of responsibilities.

If you haven't noticed, there is a method to this.

We started by making a list and scheduling that list.

Then we made another list and scheduled that list.

This method will help you no matter what you need to structure or order. A list is just a list. Once your list has a date and time, it becomes an executable item.

On the next few pages, you will see an example of a weekly schedule with priorities and responsibilities. Priorities are bold. Again, this is a modified example of what a week may look like for me. I know that not everyone is married with kids and doing the things that I do, so adjust this to fit your life's current season.

MONDAY

5:00 AM-6:00 AM	Fitness (Gym)	Priority
6:00 AM-7:00 AM	Reading/Prayer	Priority
7:30 AM-8:30 AM	Take kids to school	Responsibility
8:30 AM-2:30 PM	Work	Priority
2:30 PM-3:30 PM	Pick up kids from school	Responsibility
3:30 PM-5:00 PM	Grocery Shopping	Responsibility
5:00 PM-7:00 PM	Dinner/Dance Class	Responsibility
7:00 PM-9:00 PM	Homework with kids	Responsibility

TUESDAY

5:00 AM-6:00 AM	Fitness (Run)	Priority
6:00 AM-7:00 AM	Reading/Prayer	Priority
7:30 AM-8:30 AM	Take kids to school	Responsibility
8:30 AM-2:30 PM	Work	Priority
2:30 PM-3:30 PM	Pick up kids from school	Responsibility
3:30 PM-5:00 PM	Homework with kids	Responsibility
5:00 PM-7:00 PM	Dinner/Sports Practice	Responsibility
7:00 PM-8:00 PM	Coffee with a friend	Responsibility
8:00 PM-9:00 PM	Pay bills / personal filing	Responsibility

WEDNESDAY

5:00 AM-6:00 AM	Fitness (Gym)	Priority
6:00 AM-7:00 AM	Reading/Prayer	Priority
7:30 AM-8:30 AM	Take kids to school	Responsibility
8:30 AM-2:30 PM	Work	Priority
2:30 PM-3:30 PM	Pick up kids from school	Responsibility
3:30 PM-5:00 PM	Homework with kids	Responsibility
5:00 PM-6:30 PM	Dinner with family	Priority
7:00 PM-9:00 PM	Church	Priority

THURSDAY

5:00 AM-6:00 AM	Fitness (Run)	Priority
6:00 AM-7:00 AM	Reading/Prayer	Priority
7:30 AM-8:30 AM	Take kids to school	Responsibility
8:30 AM-2:30 PM	Work	Priority
2:30 PM-3:30 PM	Pick up kids from school	Responsibility
3:30 PM-5:00 PM	Homework with kids	Responsibility
5:00 PM-10:00 PM	Date Night	Priority
10:00 PM-10:30 PM	Pay bills / personal filing	Responsibility

FRIDAY

5:00 AM-6:00 AM	Fitness (Gym)	Priority
6:00 AM-7:00 AM	Reading/Prayer	Priority
7:30 AM-8:30 AM	Take kids to school	Responsibility
8:30 AM-2:30 PM	Errands / Domestic chores	Responsibility
2:30 PM-3:30 PM	Pick up kids from school	Responsibility
5:00 PM-10:00 PM	Family Night	Priority

SATURDAY

I devote Saturdays to my family, errands, honey-dos, and occasionally relaxing. This is also a time for maximizing my "nickel and dime" moments to make things intentional with what matters most (see STEP 5).

SUNDAY

My family and I are involved in church, so we set aside this day for that as well as family time, errands, honey-dos, and some occasional relaxing. I also use this time to maximize my "nickel and dime" moments to make things intentional with what matters most (see STEP 5).

Step 5 | Nickle and Dime It

*"Battles are won by slaughter and maneuver.
The greater the general, the more he contributes in maneuver,
the less he demands in slaughter."*
—Winston Churchill

Once you have everything you need intentionally scheduled in your calendar – it's not over yet. You will need to get intentional with your time, finding minutes here and there to spend doing things you need to do that day. Have you ever had to search the house for loose change to pay for something because you couldn't find your wallet or maybe didn't have the money? You frantically searched everywhere in sight. Every nickel and dime you found was like gold and added up to get you what you desired.

Especially when you were a kid and the ice cream truck was driving down your street. I remember being inside or outside – it didn't matter – and I would hear that music playing from blocks away. I would panic, knowing I had to find money quickly to get my Johnny Apple Treats candy and a Flintstones Push-Up Pop. I would run to my mom (because dad was at work) and ask for some change. She would always direct me to her purse, which never seemed to be where she said it was. I would finally find it and grab every nickel and dime I could. Then, I would throw off the couch cushions and dig in the cracks of the couch, looking for more. I would check the family car ashtray and every junk drawer in the house. Every nickel and every dime were getting me one step closer to what I wanted most – ice cream!

So, let's think for a moment in terms of nickels and dimes with our time – nickels represent five minutes, and dimes represent 10 minutes. When you can find an extra 10 minutes, it's like gold in your day – especially if it's for a quick nap or some alone time. I call this milking your day for all it's worth.

Let me give you another example of this in my own life.

On Mondays, I have a priority to study and prepare for speaking events. That takes up a few hours, but I also use that day as a reset from the busy weekend. So, I run small errands on that day and use my time in the truck to call clients and follow up on their progress. My truck is a nickel and dime moment of my day. I know it doesn't sound like much of a day off, but it's my version of one (ha-ha). You could easily waste a 15-minute car ride listening to music. But I intentionally take advantage of that nickel (five minutes) and dime (ten minutes) and redirect them toward a **PRIORITY** of mine.

Remember, priorities are what matters most to you in life. Since personal growth is one of my priorities, I can easily take a 15-minute drive and turn my truck into a classroom while listening to an audiobook or podcast that helps feed my personal growth.

Are you beginning to see how *Calendar Hacking* works now?

Intentionality is always more profitable than intentions. Many people intend to do something but never do it. Being intentional will ensure things get done.

I told you earlier that family time and a date night with my wife are priorities to me. I cannot do both in one day, so I determined to be home every night and be intentional in my time to invest in my kids. This may mean that I choose to get gas later that night instead of during my daily errands so that I can find a dime of my time to take one of my kids with me to the gas station. Candy and soda with dad creates memories that will last a lifetime. Occasionally, I will find a few dimes in my day, and I'll save them up for an impromptu lunch or coffee date with my wife. These are golden. Anything out of the norm to show that I have time for my wife and kids really goes a long way.

One day I arrived at a local coffee shop to meet a coaching client. As I always do, I glanced over my calendar to make sure I knew what intentionally scheduled things followed. This particular coaching session was a one-hour session starting at noon. I noticed that my next appointment wasn't until 1:30. That was three dimes!!! I know that had I not looked at my calendar with the intent to "nickel and dime" my time, I would have allowed my coaching session to bleed over into that unscheduled thirty minutes. I would have missed the opportunity to milk that day of every possible minute. I quickly went through my list of priorities in my mind to find one in which I could invest the newly discovered three dimes (30 minutes). I texted my wife to see where she was. She was on her way to a nail salon nearby to get her nails done. Aha, this was my moment.

So, I went inside the coffee shop to meet my client and said to them, *"It's so good to see you. I am excited about our time together today. I want to remind you that we set aside one hour to accomplish your goals today. I have another meeting following this one, so I want to make the most of our time together today by letting you start by telling me what you'd like to discuss today."* My client knew that I would be getting up from the table at 1:00 PM. That was intentional.

After our session ended, I shook hands with my client and made my way to the barista to order my wife's favorite drink. I ordered myself another coffee, too, and headed to the nail salon to surprise my wife. I walked in with coffees in hand, and you would have thought I bought her a new car. She smiled from ear to ear and asked, *"Babe, what are you doing here?"* I said, *"Well, I know how much you like your Pumpkin Spice Latte, and I found an extra thirty minutes in my day, so I wanted to spend it with you."* The ladies in the salon went wild. *"Girl, my man doesn't even know what my favorite drink is, much less take time off of work to bring me one."* My wife blushed and felt like the most important woman in the room. And rightfully so – she was.

My intentional *Calendar Hacking* helped solidify that in her heart at that moment. She is my queen, and she is my priority. Your day has nickels and dimes hidden throughout it. All you have to do is look for them.

You cannot milk a day that you don't have structured. Simply looking at your calendar will help you see a 30-minute gap between scheduled things that can be harnessed and redirected towards a priority. Take that time and milk it. If not, you will extend a responsibility and eat up free time that you could use for something of greater value.

Get creative when it comes to investing in relationships that matter to you. As a father, I have found some very unique ways of doing this. There was a season of my life where I worked non-stop and slept very little, causing time to slip from my hands, and I missed out on important times with my kids. Even more devastating, they missed out on important times with me.

Relationships go both ways – each party supplies and receives a need to/from each other. For Christmas one year, we bought electric scooters for all of our kids who were old enough to ride them. My wife asked me what I wanted for Christmas. Because money was tight, I said, *"Babe, I'm good. Let's just get the kids what they want."* She said, *"Well, my mom and dad asked me what you wanted for Christmas, so let me know, and I'll tell them so they can get you something."* I needed at least 100 things, but what I desired more than anything was more time with my kids. So, I searched online for a motorized scooter that could hold my body weight, and I told my wife that was what I wanted. At Christmas that year, my in-laws cracked jokes about me wanting such an adolescent present. They had no idea the internal anguish I was carrying by not investing the time into my kids that I wanted to.

As I was still figuring out how to hack my calendar, I would often take spontaneous breaks from working at my office (my dining room table), and I would holler to my kids, *"Who wants to ride scooters with dad?"* They would jump up, and we would all rush to the garage to take a scooter ride. These memories I will never forget. Grabbing five or ten minutes here and there to invest in my kids was like gold. There was a gas station not too far from our house, and we would frequently pile on my scooter like circus clowns and cautiously ride there for sodas, chips, and the kids' favorite candy. To this day, my kids still talk about our gas station trips on the scooter. I am so thankful that I didn't ask for a new coat or a new laptop for Christmas. Neither of those would have drawn me closer to my kids or helped me invest in them.

Find creative ways that force you to invest in what matters most. When you do, you will see a return on those investments. You may not see it immediately, but you will see it eventually. The opposite is true too. You may not see the immediate result of neglecting to invest your time into what matters most, but you can be confident it will reveal itself one day. Just ask the many adults in therapist's offices right now because they did not have a parent in their life to instill within them the traits needed later in life to cope with difficulties and challenges.

This may sound extreme, but I have sat across the table of many grown men and women who, with tears streaming down their face, tell me about how their father or mother wasn't there for them. Don't let this be you. I am so thankful that I caught it early in my kids' lives. I have seen a few things pop up during their teenage years, but my life was balanced and healthy, so I could deal with it before it got out of hand. And yours will be, too, through applying these proven *Calendar Hacking* steps. As I said, I have lived these and have seen the power they have on the success of not just a day, but in the quality of life.

No White Space Allowed

*"I believe every human has a finite number of heartbeats.
I don't intend to waste any of mine."*
–Neil Armstrong

If you are like me, you prefer everything digital and synced. I choose a cloud version of any app.

I will say, however, that when it comes to books, I am still old school and prefer a hardcover so I can underline and highlight text. But for my calendar, my iPhone is the only thing I trust to keep me on schedule.

I color-code the activities scheduled on my calendar as follows:

- Personal – Blue
- Business – Red
- Family – Yellow

Once my day is scheduled, I can look at my day view and see the horizontal color bars fill the screen. In between the bars, there is usually white space.

Let me explain. Let's say I had a one-hour meeting with a client at noon. Because it is for my business, it will be color-coded in red. If I have a personal event, like picking up my kids from school at 1:30 PM, that would be labeled blue. In between those two events (red and blue), would be a white space. That white space represents 30 minutes of unscheduled and unintentional time. This is where the "nickel and dime it" step comes in.

AVOID WHITE SPACE IN YOUR CALENDAR

I'm not telling you to busy yourself all day and never sleep. I am telling you to give every space on your calendar a name.

When I coach my clients, we dive headfirst together into their entire life. We spend a good bit of time in the financial lane, helping them determine the quality of life they desire and what it will take to get them there.

We usually start by eliminating debt. With debt cancellation strategies, many financial advisors (I am not a financial advisor) suggest giving every dollar a name. That is wisdom, and if you haven't ever done this, you MUST do this.

Let me break it down for you. If you make $10,000 a month and your bills are $8,000 a month, most people would be like, *"Wow, I have an extra $2,000 to spend however I want."* No, this is a lie. If you treat unallotted money as "free money," you will find ways to spend it quickly that will never add any real value to your life or financial future. It will be as if it just disappeared. So, every dollar must have a name. If your mortgage is $2,500 per month, then $2,500 of that $10,000 made is named "Mortgage." If your cell phone is $150 per month, then $150 of that $10,000 is called "Cell Phone." Are you beginning to see it? So, if you have

$2,000 in unallocated funds and you have a plan to pay off debt, then those "extra" $2,000 immediately is labeled *"Pay Off Debt."*

I encourage you to use this same strategy with your time. Every minute MUST have a name, even if that name is *"Sleep."* That's right; my calendar has blue events labeled "Wake Up" and others marked "Bedtime." Be so intentional with everything you do that you have milked your day for everything it had. Any left-over time or white space in your calendar should go towards a listed priority first, and then if you have anything left, you can delegate it to a responsibility that demands more attention.

There are times when I will look at my calendar specifically to see if there are white spaces, and then I will label them *read a book, run a mile, spend time with my wife, take a nap, stare at the wall,* etc. I am so adamant about not having white space that I will hunt for it throughout the week to see what unscheduled and unintentional time I can use by intentionally giving it a name and scheduling it.

So, after you have done all five of the steps to *Calendar Hacking*, make sure you continually tweak your calendar throughout the day to ensure no white space gets unnoticed.

Live this way for 12 weeks, and your life will never be the same.

This works whether you work for a business or own one and whether you make $30,000 per year or $3,000,000.

Remember, time is NOT money – time is *FREEDOM*. And people who have more money usually find a way to have more freedom. People who view time as money often value things that produce money rather than something that produces life. With the "time is money" mindset, time spent with your kids is viewed as a waste because it doesn't make you any money.

Some men refuse to take family vacations and spend much-needed time with their family because they know if they keep working, they will make more money. They often believe that once they make the money, they will have the finances and budget to take their family somewhere nice. The truth is though, once work becomes your habit, time with family will not.

I choose to invest my time rather than spending my time. Years ago, when my wife and I first got married, we would have another young married couple over to our house each week. We enjoyed having others in our lives that shared the same season of life as us. Plus, who doesn't like having friends, right? As months went on, I took inventory of our times together. Every time they came over, I noticed that they complained about other people and disagreed with almost everything everyone else was doing or said. It became very draining.

One night I said to my wife, *"Babe, I know she is your friend, but I have to say I feel like our time with them is spent and not invested. I think we should cut back on the time we spend with them."* We both agreed and decided to have them over less. Now that we are no longer in a relationship with them, they are at other people's houses talking about us.

> *You see, time spent is gone forever. Time invested has an ROI. Any good investment has a return on investment.*

If you are filling your schedule with things that you *spend* your time on, those are expensive things. I told my wife that night, "*Our relationship with this couple is costly. It is time spent and not invested. We should find another couple we can invest our time in, and they can invest in us so that we all gain from the relationship.*

My Secret Move

What I am about to tell you will completely change your life.

When it comes to *Calendar Hacking* my own life and preserving my mental health, my secret move is a trick I call *Front-loading*. I front-load my weeks so that my weekends are free to invest more intentional time and energy into my family.

My family is the top priority in my life, so I make sure they get as much of my time as possible. Most people hate Mondays, but I am the complete opposite. I love Mondays, almost in a weird way. Heck, I love to work, period. I am wired to be busy all of the time, but I had to learn to turn my busyness into productiveness. When others ask me how my day was, I used to say, *"I had a very busy day."* Now, I have replaced my response with, *"I had a very productive day."*

I front-load my weeks so that most of my tasks are accomplished early in the week, diminishing my workload as the week goes on. For example, let's think in terms of the percentage of work by days. On the next page is an idea of what my week would look like in terms of responsibility. Again, I do not have unscheduled or allotted times on the weekend. I choose not to have commitments or tasks on those days and redirect my time to my family.

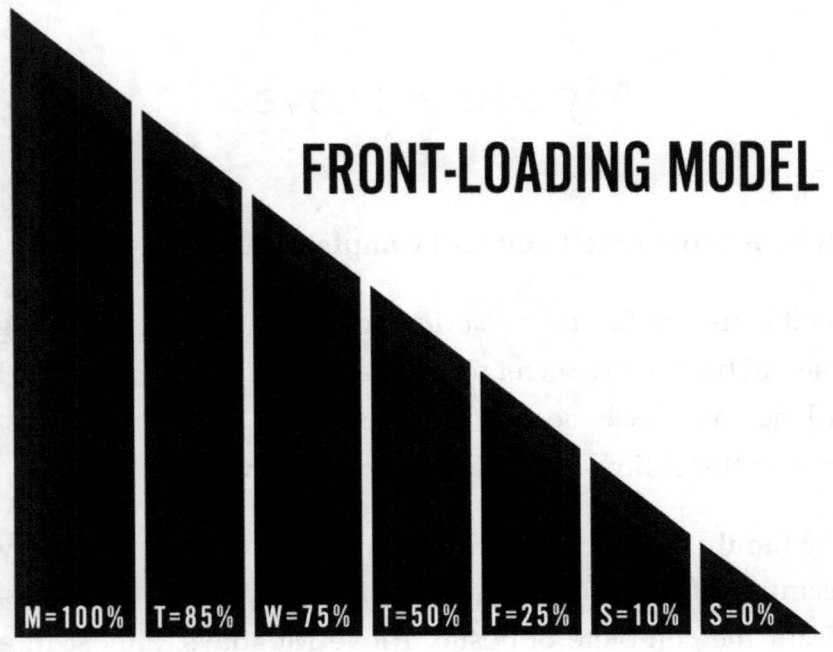

Monday	=	100%
Tuesday	=	85%
Wednesday	=	75%
Thursday	=	50%
Friday	=	25%
Saturday	=	10%
Sunday	=	0%

If you think of it as a slope, my week would be high on Monday and low on Sunday. I like to picture myself as a skier headed towards my goal of family time at the end of the slope.

Do you see how this can make for a productive few days at the start of the week and some restful days at the end of the week?

What matters most to me gets the most of me when we are together. I don't want my wife getting 10% of me on our date because my day got the other 90%.

Make sense?

I also am the head coach of all my kid's sports teams. I found favor with the sports organization because they were in desperate need of more coaches and were pleased that I stepped up and coached so many. That favor allowed me the unique privilege of holding weekly practices around my schedule. That was gold for me because I front-loaded them in my week so I could spend my weekend with my family. With my weeks front-loaded like they are, it also gives me the freedom for weekend getaways with my wife or family, as well as impromptu speaking opportunities that pop up.

When you get really good at *Calendar Hacking*, you will feel like a puppet master controlling your days like a pro.

Adapt With The Seasons

I've been pretty transparent about my shortcomings with you in this book. I have to be honest with you though, just because I know how to *Calendar Hack* doesn't mean that it's automatic for me.

Let me explain.

As you get skilled at mastering your calendar, it's incredible how your life will flow and operate at a whole new level.

Hear me when I tell you this, you MUST evaluate yourself and your calendar constantly.

Sometimes what we "give up to go up" is necessary for that particular season. However, that doesn't mean that every season will mimic the previous one. We must add things to our lives to sustain and excel at higher levels of success.

As I said before, I run multiple businesses. One business, in particular, was a life-long dream of mine. I was honored to share it with my wife and significantly made an impact in our industry locally and globally. It became so successful that others in our industry began calling us, asking if they could fly in and see how we did what we did. They even asked if we would visit their businesses – all expenses paid – and consult with their teams on changes they could make to achieve success similar to what we were experiencing. Things were going amazingly well. Then, just like anything that is growing, we experienced growing pains.

I continued to hack my calendar, but I neglected to add a much-needed priority – *myself*. I needed to make myself a priority and schedule time for rest and recovery from my grueling schedule. I was speaking weekly and traveling to different states and countries monthly. I had requests to appear on television programs, radio programs, podcasts, speak at and host large conferences, and even write forewords for books.

Seems amazing, right?

It was, but also was slowly and unknowingly draining me to a place I never thought I would be. Through all this success, my kids were growing older, and I was growing busier. Sure, we had our family nights and "nickel and dimed" our time together like pros, but the momentum and acceleration of success were sucking the life out of me, and I didn't know how to get it back. In this season, I co-founded a network for non-profits around the globe. It quickly took off and added an extra twenty to thirty hours a week to my plate of intense work and mental focus.

Did I mention this was voluntary?

That's right. I did it for free. I am a huge advocate for using your gifts, talents, and resources to help others and add value to them. But what I didn't realize was that I was hurting myself the whole time I was helping everyone else. I felt that I needed a break, but when I sat and reasoned it out in my mind, I determined that it was best to keep going and get through it and rest and recover later. That was a bad idea. If you have ever flown commercially, you have sat through the flight attendant's demonstration of the rules and procedures you are to follow in case of an emergency. They always say that oxygen masks will lower from the plane's overhead bin in case of a decrease in cabin pressure. They instruct you to put your oxygen mask on first before helping others. Why? Because if you are dead, how can you help others who need help? I should have done this, but I was helping everyone else with their issues, and it hindered me the most.

When you are depleted, you make decisions and do things that you usually wouldn't do, which happened to me. Through my neglect and failure to rest and practice self-care, I found myself on my mentor's living room couch, holding my wife's hand as we decided to close the business.

It had come to this: either I lose my marriage and my family and keep the business, or I close it, take some much-needed time off and repair what I had unknowingly wrecked for over a decade – myself and my family.

Closing the business was the hardest thing I had ever done, but I truly believe closing a marriage and a family would have been even harder.

Maybe this sounds familiar to you, or perhaps you know someone who resembles this story. Many view calendars as a piece of paper with dates on them, but it is much more than that.

A calendar is a blank canvas that allows you to choose what colors and images make it into the picture you are painting. If your family doesn't look the way you want it to right now, stop painting it that way. Before it's too late, clear the canvas (your calendar) and intentionally add to the picture the things you desire to see.

Yes, there are only twenty-four hours in a day, but we can choose who and what gets each minute. Give those minutes to the people and things that matter the most to you.

- How's your mental health?
- How's your marriage?
- How's your relationship with your kids?
- How's your relationship with God?
- When is the last time you went to a movie by yourself just because you could and wanted some alone time?
- Do you wish you had more friends?
- Why haven't you taken the time to schedule a guys' night or girls' night out with your friends and start having a social life that allows you to expand your social network?

I have had the privilege of being in the hospital room with people who were moments away from dying. I shared my heart and gratitude with them and expressed how much they meant to me and how much I would miss them. In every single instance, the dying person wished they had more time. Steward what you have so intentionally that it feels like you are gaining time rather than losing it.

Calendar Hacking Praise

I want to share a few testimonials from clients who went through my *Calendar Hacking* method and tell how it affected their lives as a whole. These are just a few of the many clients I have worldwide who have benefitted from this minimalistic approach to time management and productivity habits. I would love to hear about your experience as you go through this same life-changing method. Please write us and let us know how your life and success progress along the way.

Visit CalendarHackingBook.com to share your testimony.

Testimonial #1: Wife, Mother of Four, Entrepreneur and CEO.

"By nature, I am laid back, some would say to a fault. Structure and routine are necessary for me to live a productive life and is vital to my success. I have always had my hand in more things I can count at one time! I love people, but quickly realized that the time I was giving to these people seemed limited and tired. It was through Caleb's Calendar Hacking that I learned how to not just create space for everything I wanted to do but add value to the time I dedicated to those things. Prior to learning from Caleb, my calendar resembled more of a running list of tasks that I would often have to shift to the following days because those items didn't have scheduled times and usually didn't get completed.

First and foremost, I am a wife and mom of four; those five people directly need me and my time often. They are priority! I didn't like the feeling that my priorities were getting the water-downed version of what they should have been getting in and from me. I have a growth mindset, so I'm constantly looking to grow in every area of my life to elevate to the best version of myself. I desire to continually grow spiritually and advance my relationship with God, invest in my friendships and community, remain a figure in the non-profit sector both locally and nationally, grow and scale my fitness coaching business, and elevate my own fitness levels through marathon racing. I love adventure and trying new things. It's also in my personality to want to do everything and do it well. Wrap all of that into one and place the bow of personal dreams and goals on top and you have the previous me - a tired and stretched too thin wife, mom, and business owner.

What I loved most about Caleb's proven method was he didn't tell me to just lighten my load, as people had in the past. He – like me – was maintaining successful relationships and continuing to scale his successful business, along with personal dreams and goals. Caleb simply walked me through prioritizing what was best and then scheduling from there. Since in my youth, I have always had the mindset that I could actually DO IT ALL and do it all well. I still believe that for myself. I was stuck running around only to give those most important people and things in my life a lesser version than they deserved.

When hiring Caleb and his company for coaching, consulting, and marketing for my business, I knew not only his talents and experience were desired and needed to build and scale my business, but that his structure and attention to detail was an added benefit. He doesn't just teach his method, he lives it! After greatly benefiting from Caleb's proven Calendar Hacking methods, I decided that it was too life-changing not to share with my clients! I help moms gain confidence by reaching their fitness goals and I wanted to help change the hundreds of moms' lives around the world with the exact same things that had changed my life! I now use his Calendar Hacking method with all my clients and have easily adapted it into one of the first steps of my client's transformation process. I'm able to help moms find more time in their days, just as I had, become more structured and organized and show them that they can wear all of the many hats moms do and not be overwhelmed. It's so simple and minimalistic, anyone can do it!

I have gone from aspiring to juggle life and business to ACTUALLY having life and business coexist well. Prior to walking through Caleb's Calendar Hacking method, I would say to others that I "thrive in chaos," I now confidently and simply say, "I thrive!" Our lives don't have to be chaotic; we are the owners and dictators of our time, and Calendar Hacking proved that."

Testimonial #2: Wife, Mother of Five, Podcaster, Itinerate Speaker, Influencer, Coach, Entrepreneur and CEO.

"I can't even begin to tell you what a difference Calendar Hacking has made in my life! As a wife, mother of five, and an entrepreneur, I felt like I was drowning every single day just trying to keep up with it all. It has always been my desire to be the best wife and the best mom I could possibly be, which didn't seem to leave much room for personal goals or agenda. Being the "best mom" or "best wife" can be fully loaded with unreasonable expectations from both society and ourselves. Not to mention having my own dreams and desires for my life that have steadfastly remained on the backburner for the past 15 years.

How could it ever be possible for me to chase, much less achieve my dreams while raising a family well? This was the question that haunted me and kept me "idle" for many years. I felt like I had to choose between family devotion and devotion to my dreams. Then, I was introduced to Caleb's Calendar Hacking system! It has been a total game-changer in the way I do life and to the life I get to live.

Before Calendar Hacking, I took every day as it came. I was constantly on and off-task, not completing tasks, and definitely couldn't find time to pursue my dreams. I mean, I couldn't finish a load of laundry without being distracted with a million other things along the way, much less get beyond these little tasks into something that I felt would make a difference in the world.

By no means am I making little of the job of a full-time homemaker! It is not for the faint of heart and should be the highest paying job around. However, if you have other aspirations in your heart beyond homemaking, it is possible!

To all the moms out there that have a dream – maybe you want to start your own business, work in direct sales, write a book, open a restaurant, get your certification in fitness, start a side hustle that lets you travel or do the things you've always wanted to do – you don't have to choose between your family and your dream.

My husband was actually the first "believer" in Caleb's system. He is a product of and advocate for the Calendar Hacking system, and I can tell you first-hand how much it has made a difference in his life. The way he fathers our children to the way he makes time to invest in our marriage has made a world of difference. He used to work all day, come home and pull out the laptop and work until late at night. He had no time for the kids and me, hobbies, or his health. Incorporating this system has given him the proper boundaries between work, home, health, and relationships. I always knew his heart was to provide well for his family, and that is why he worked endless hours, but I also knew how much he loved his family and wanted to spend time with them. I hated seeing him struggling to juggle business and life- and trying to succeed at both.

The pressure and stress weighed on him constantly, and he just didn't know how to balance it all. It has been amazing to see how just by taking the steps he learned in Calendar Hacking and applying them to his life and schedule has not only afforded him the time for his family, health and relationships, but he is a very successful entrepreneur! Wow! Doing life AND business well! I was sold right away and couldn't wait *to put this same system into practice in my own life and calendar. I was blown away at how much I could fit into my day without feeling overwhelmed or like I was drowning.*

I have learned proper time management, how to identify my priorities, how to list my responsibilities, and execute it all with more ease than ever. Because of this method, I started my own Podcast, I travel and speak all across America, and I am working on my very first book! I am NO LONGER in "idle," nor are my dreams on the back burner. This is the deal, we all get this one life to live. I don't want to live with regret. I don't want to get to the end of my life and wish I would have done all the things that were in my heart to do — and I definitely don't want to come to the realization that what kept me from it was too much laundry!!!

I want to shout from the roof tops about this system. It is my personal belief that EVERYONE needs to get acquainted with Caleb's Calendar Hacking and put it into practice in their lives. If you want to live well and love well, this system is for you!"

Testimonial #3: Husband, Father of Seven, Entrepreneur, and CEO

"Before I met Caleb, my life was a mess. From my career to my marriage, I couldn't figure out how any of it was going to work out. It seemed giving up was the best option for everything I was involved in. I was even failing at being a dad. I had two businesses that I was juggling, but neither seemed to be going anywhere. Then I met Caleb and was introduced to Calendar Hacking. At first, I thought, "Scheduling things in my calendar is not going to help my failing life, marriage, family, or businesses." Man, was I wrong! Within days, I saw a massive difference in my life and began seeing my marriage, family, and business pivot and head towards success for the first time in a long time. As I continued to use the steps he teaches, I began to find more time in my days and weeks that I never knew had been available for years. My business tripled within one year, and my marriage was better than ever.

My wife and I had another child and started another business along the way. Now, I could end the story hear and it would be great, but I feel I need to be transparent and honest. I had seen such great success and had grown so much through Caleb's coaching and his proven Calendar Hacking method that I unintentionally set my life and success to autopilot mode. Then, without warning, I found myself in a worse place than when I first met Caleb. My marriage was at an all-time low, my kids resented me, all three of my businesses were on the brink of bankruptcy and closing their doors, my personal health was the worst ever, my mental health was toxic, and my finances were shameful. I was ready to call it quits. If I'm being honest, suicidal was more like it.

I called Caleb one day and gave him the blunt pulse of where I was at that moment and he asked me, "How is your calendar?" At first, I thought, "Dude, did you not hear all the crap I just said to you that has been going on in my life?" But then it hit me, I had gotten away from the routine and habit of tweaking my calendar daily and forecasting my weeks and months like he taught me in our coaching sessions. He then asked me, "When was your life more successful than it is right now?" I sheepishly told him, "When I was applying the 5 Steps to a Productive Week in your Calendar Hacking method." And like a good coach, Caleb said, "Well, seems like you already have the answer to your problems and the tools needed to get the job done."

It took no time at all to see my life do a 180 and get back on route toward better and brighter days for me, my marriage, my family, and my career. I have seen the before and after of the Calendar Hacking method, and the after is always better – trust me. I also know what it's like to taste the success of Caleb's program only to revisit the taste of failure and decline that I had all those years before hiring him. It was like riding a bicycle – I got right back on and picked it back up as if I had never gotten off in the first place. This method works, and it works every time. I would not be where I am today if it had not been for taking the desperate leap of faith into something so simple yet so powerful. I have even started taking my kids through the steps and they are seeing greater results as well. Thank you, Caleb, for all your help, you have truly changed my life (a few times)."

Testimonial #4: Single Father of One, Podcaster, Entrepreneur, and CEO

"When I met Caleb, I would say I felt successful as a man in many areas. I had already created a life for myself that most men would dream of. I had a nice house, owned and operated many successful businesses, had lots of money and toys – but my priorities were off. My relationship with my son was toxic. I was working so hard and literally all of the time that I lived on the edge – carrying much stress and anxiety home with me each day. This would cause me to snap at my son for the smallest of things. I could tell that it was crushing his spirit and hurting our bond. Within just a few coaching sessions with Caleb, he began to talk to me about Calendar Hacking. At first, I thought to myself, "Adding more things to my calendar is the LAST thing I need right now."

Then, Caleb explained to me that it wasn't about adding more to my schedule or plate, but about determining what will get the majority of my time and why. He helped me truly understand the difference between a priority and a responsibility and set boundaries in my life through my calendar that would ensure I got the most out of each day and scheduled moment. I can honestly say that this healed my relationship with my son and me. He is living with a brand-new dad and we are loving the time we spend together. The 5 Steps to a Productive Week that Caleb teaches have also given me a deeper relationship with God. I never had time before for church, reading my bible, or praying. Now I do thanks to the steps I took through his coaching."

What's the Forecast?

It is easy for us to isolate ourselves and conclude that we are the only person dealing with what we are going through, and no one will ever understand or relate. This is false. Many others are in worse circumstances than you yet have a positive outlook on their life. They are experiencing success despite their situation. It's been said, *"Life is what we make it."* I would like to add another perspective to that,

---

"Life is how we schedule it."

Asking yourself, *"How do I want to live my life tomorrow?"* will help you capture moments that would otherwise go unnoticed. To effectively live today, you must have intentionally put the plan together in advance. Forecasting your days, weeks, months, quarters, and even years is essential.

Only a fool would plan a trip while en route. Make plans beforehand to be best prepared for what lies in the days ahead. Take some time today to think about tomorrow. Look at what is scheduled on your calendar for tomorrow and predict how the day will go. Will you need to push a meeting or task back 10 or

15 minutes? Will you need to extend a priority an extra 30 minutes? Do you see a possible conflict and need to reschedule an event to another day to give it the proper attention it needs?

By forecasting your days and week, you will be able to spot unforeseen challenges and make the necessary adjustments ahead of time to keep your life flowing with ease. I frequently have to make adjustments to my calendar. For example, my wife and I have a date night every Thursday, but sometimes an unforeseen event is thrown into our perfectly scheduled life, so we have to pivot.

My calendar is boss, and I MUST obey it if it tells me I have a date night with my wife. So, what do I do when worlds collide? I adjust. I look at my calendar and see that I have white space Sunday night, so I move date night to Sunday for that week instead of canceling it. I move events around like a Tetris game. I am creative and skilled at manipulating time for my benefit and success. And my wife knows she is still a priority.

Forecasting is next-level stuff. If you can get good at forecasting, you will have a secure and worry-free future. You can lay your head on your pillow at night knowing that the next day is set up for your success.

Now, I must tell you that bringing order to your life may cause frustration. Let me explain.

When one member of a disorganized family gets organized, it can cause frustration. It's like cleaning your car, and your kids mess it up again. The other day, I spent hundreds of dollars getting my truck detailed for a hunting trip with some colleagues. Twenty minutes later, I had to take my kids to an event. My youngest son got in the truck with a carton of chocolate milk and spilled it all over the back seat, floor mats, center console, and it splashed up on the front two seats. I was frustrated to say the least. But this is exactly what happens when I take a client through these *Calendar Hacking* steps. He or she will come back to me and say, *"I see the value in it, and I know it is working, but it is nearly impossible to sustain because my spouse is such a free spirit and my kids do not have a routine or schedule."*

You will experience frustration at times; however, you can push through it and continue to structure your bliss in the midst of others' chaos.

My advice: Do the steps with your spouse or significant other. This is what helped my wife and me. I made my schedule, and we reviewed it together to see if I had included anything unrealistic or if I had overlooked anything. We immediately found a conflict, so we each tweaked our calendars. We decided to live that calendar to the minute for one whole week, and then we met to discuss the results. We both found it transformational in our time and saw where we needed to make a few adjustments. Of course, I had to remove some of the unnecessary things I had put in my calendar.

I tend to do things in extremes. For instance, when I decide to read a book, I assume I can read it in one day. While I know that's not realistic for my life, I love the extreme challenge and think I can do it. My wife helps to dial it back saying, *"Babe, why don't you start with a book a month and see how that goes first."* And that is the wisdom I need in my corner always.

So, as you set out on this journey to improve the quality of your life and mind, remember to be patient with yourself and others while you work out the kinks. And don't be afraid to make edits along the way. Here's to the new you. You are going to love your new life and new self.

5 Steps to a Productive Week – Recap

1. Make a list of your weekly priorities.

2. Spread out the tasks on your list throughout the week by intentionally scheduling each priority on your calendar.

3. Make a list of your responsibilities.

4. Fill in all available time slots on your calendar with your responsibilities.

5. Get the most out of your day/week by finding unscheduled or unallotted moments and redirecting them towards a priority.

This proven *Calendar Hacking* skill will save your marriage, your family, and even your life. Too many people are depressed, stressed, anxious, unhappy, worried, unfulfilled… the list goes on – because they do not hold the reigns of their calendar or day.

Now that you have these five *Calendar Hacking* Steps to a Productive Week take what you have learned and UNDERwhelm what has been overwhelming you for so long.

Resources For Your Toolbox

Everybody has a preferred method to organize tasks and appointments. I prefer to use my iPhone calendar and Notes app. Below is a list of several excellent resources you can utilize to help manage your days, weeks, months, and years. Review the features of each tool to determine if you could benefit from using any of these. New apps and programs are continually being designed, so stay connected to what's out there so that you can keep evolving in efficiency.

Trello

Trello is a digital bulletin board that you can customize to organize to-do lists, mark tasks, and make notes.

With Trello, you can create lists, which are dynamic containers that you can fill with cards that include notes, tasks, thoughts, pictures, and more. You can move cards within a list or move them to other lists.

Using Trello, you can share thoughts and tasks with other users, make new cards, add comments, and assign tasks.

24me

24me is an amazing virtual assistant app that helps you organize your hectic days with features such as notes, a to-do list, and a calendar that syncs with several other calendar services (Outlook, iCal, Google Calendar, etc.).

24me allows you to set up notifications, event and task reminders, and traffic and weather alerts.

Voice control features enable you to set appointments and take notes in a breeze. You can also create tasks using external devices like Siri, Alexa, etc.

Any.do

If you tend to get so busy that you easily forget to do daily chores, then Any.do is a great tool for you. The app provides a to-do list, notes, and reminders to keep you conscious of everything that you need to do.

The app allows you to share your lists with or assign tasks to others. You can sync your lists between web, desktop, and mobile platforms, allowing you to update your lists in real time. The voice entry feature enables you to quickly add items by speaking.

Todoist

Todoist is another amazing multi-platform planner and to-do list app that allows you to easily transform a written thought into a one-time task or recurring task.

Other features include color-coded priority levels, shared projects, and productivity graphs to help you keep track of your progress.

Memento

iPhone users can use this app for a more aesthetically-pleasing view of reminders and upcoming tasks.

Memento also appears as a widget and includes a "For You" tab that provides an at-a-glance of your most important reminders.

About the Author

As an influencer to influencers, Caleb W. Moran is a #1 best-selling author, coach, and international speaker. From one-on-one sessions to speaking on stage in front of thousands, his simple yet charismatic approach to leadership, business, and the Bible has captivated audiences for decades. Often referred to as "The Entrepreneur Midwife," he is passionate about helping people give birth to their entrepreneurial dreams.

Caleb is the founder and CEO of The 400 Company, working with elite companies and executive leadership around the globe to help individuals, leaders, and organizations scale to operate at new levels.

With a passion for philanthropy, Caleb teaches individuals and organizations his proven methods to increase and create revenue streams to use wealth to influence and change the world around them.

Notes

Notes

Notes

Notes

Notes

Notes

Notes

Notes

Notes

Notes

Notes

Notes

Notes

Notes

www.ingramcontent.com/pod-product-compliance
Lightning Source LLC
LaVergne TN
LVHW020935090426
835512LV00020B/3367